T0079935

THE DIMINISHING HOUSE

THE DIMINISHING HOUSE

NICKY BEER

CARNEGIE MELLON UNIVERSITY PRESS
PITTSBURGH 2010

ACKNOWLEDGMENTS

Grateful acknowledgments to the editors of the journals which first published these poems, sometimes in different forms:

American Literary Review "Provenance"
Bellingham Review "1991: A List of Demands," "A Short Documentary of My Father Running Backwards"
Beloit Poetry Journal "Still Life with Half-Turned Woman and Questions," "Blue Thought/Blue Shade," "Still Life, 1656"
Cider Press Review "Variations on the Philtrum," "Patellae Apocrypha," "Ode to the Perineum," "Lobe of the Auricle"
Clackamas Literary Review "Midwife/Midsummer"
Crab Orchard Review "Genes," "My Father is a Small Submarine"
crazyhorse "Post-Mortem"
Iron Horse Literary Review "Cardinal Virtue," "Scapula," "Erosion"
Kenyon Review "Ouroboros"
Low Rent "LMNO," "His Mistress," "Season of the Drunken Wasps," "The Diminishing House"
New Orleans Review "Avuncularity," "Mako," "The Exquisite Foreplay of the Tortoise"
Notre Dame Review "To Radius and Ulna"
So to Speak "Historical Nude"
Third Coast "Annual"

"Still Life with Half-Turned Woman and Questions" appears in *Best American Poetry 2007* (Scribner). "To Radius and Ulna" appears in *Notre Dame Review: The First Ten Years* (Notre Dame UP). "Cardinal Virtue" appeared on *Verse Daily* (April 12, 2005, www.versedaily.com). I am grateful for support received as these poems were written, rewritten, and reshuffled: thanks to Inprint, Inc. for a C. Glenn Cambor Fellowship, to the University of Missouri-Columbia for a G. Ellsworth Huggins Fellowship and a Greg Lopez Scholarship in Creative Writing, and to the National Endowment for the Arts for a Literature Fellowship.

Book design: Madeleine Barnes and Kristen Staab

The publication of this book is made possible by a grant from the Pennsylvania Council on the Arts.

PENNSYLVANIA
COUNCIL
ON THE
ARTS

10   9   8   7   6   5   4   3   2   1

Page 68 constitutes an extension of this copyright page.

In memory of my father

CONTENTS

❖

THE DIMINISHING HOUSE

AVUNCULARITY

Every child ought to have a dead uncle.
There should be only one surviving photograph,
or else a handful of epochal snapshots
where the face is always blurred, in half-light,
or otherwise indistinct. Much can made of
the raised glass in his hand and the quirked
corners of his smile. And who was that girl
standing with him? Ellie? Jean? No, the one
from Pittsburgh with the dogs.
You hadn't been born then anyway. . . .
This is the one whose fault it can be:
the slight warps, the spider-cracks in your speech,
the explanation for all of the wrongness
that made the other children pause, assess you
a little coldly and pull back as one toward the playground.
Why all of the strange words seem to rise
from your tongue like damp, nocturnal creatures
into an unwelcoming light. Why you insist
on that turd-brown jacket that smells like
a musty fruitcake. Why that one thumbnail
is always gnawed to a puffed red crescent.
This man will be your phantom limb,
the thing once flesh, thrust into absence,
now living as a restless pricking under your skin,
that inward itching, that impossible,
inescapable rue fretting to itself,
the way the mouth tries to form urgent words
in a dream. And you'll take out that picture
so that your eyes can retrace the details:
red shirt, a vague mess of books
and cards on the table, half of one silver
aluminum can, a bright nova hovering
over his left shoulder as though something
has chosen that moment to rush into his body.
See, see there, his buttons are done
wrong. He must have forgotten things
all the time, just like you.

1991: A LIST OF DEMANDS

Fourteen yellowjackets scouring the weeping,
cracked face of a crabapple.

A blood-heavy sun
pitched low above an outstretched palm.

The moment when the boy's dampsilk hair
and the braille of sand on bare legs
are one thing.

Light: a six-foot scrim
of white, the hour pushing
through the dark room.

Two colors from a newly sodded lawn,
a torn-open chest releasing
bluejays and nightcrawlers.

The exact odor a sun-baked
horseshoe crab releases
when turned over with a driftwood stick.

My father's face like an obol
and two months remaining.

Wild cells shadowing the backlit
silhouette of his brain,
a fin breaching green water.

A few hundred days
soaked in gasoline, tented on timber,
set alight.

One warm gust, more caress than air,
as year passes from time to memory to ash.

An excision of all these things.

HIS MISTRESS

It was impossible to say exactly when they became acquainted—perhaps she had always been in the back of his head, shrouded by noisier thoughts the way the sun goes drab and milky when immersed in the grey cerebrums of passing cloud fronts. But as much as he neglected her through the years for the sake of husbandly pretexts, she would abide nonetheless. It was she who had given him the dark blue kimono that he wrapped around his barrel chest every morning. In the dim tedium of the Long Island Expressway she changed stations every few miles, ghosting up the windows to draw dissolving faces with her fingertip. She could always laugh at herself: the way her bad French turned *liaison* to *lesion*. One spring she wound a long blade of grass around his pinkie, which escaped his notice until bedtime, when he stared at it with utter confusion.

The first time they tried to run off together he lost his nerve. His family found him checked in as John Doe in a room that stank of antiseptic, and when he raised his head from the pillow he did not know them. He spent the next year trying to make amends, tried to excise her completely, and even after he grew pale and out of shape and lost his hair, he was shocked to learn that she still wanted him. How can anyone turn from that kind of devotion? His wife and children all required a man he no longer was; she wanted only to lie with him in the dark.

He started to take her calls again. They often found him curled in the snug box of the windowseat wearing a look of dreamy, boyish wistfulness. Soon he no longer took the trouble to finish his sentences, nor noted their puzzled worry when one of his phrases would splinter against the growing silences. And the morning finally came when all that remained was a crumpled robe on the floor like a sloughed skin and a pillow bearing the absence of his head completely full of her.

FLOATING RIB

One of the two lowest pairs of ribs,
which are attached neither to the sternum
nor to the cartilages of other ribs.

The permanent elsewhere of fathers—
my hand goes to my side as I read.
A line thrusts out into viscera, gestures
to untouchable bone. My own
private wish: to snap it free and brandish
—what? A burin? A blunderbuss?
Tool for making, unmaking. Lever
to press against my tongue, to bear me
through terrible convulsions. I will not make
of it a new body. I'll hammer it to gravel.
The rib cage opens its book, one phrase
unspeakably scrubbed.

NOTE ON THE XIPHOID PROCESS

The blunt, cartilaginous lower tip
of the sternum.

A single stalactite drips
onto the head of a blind fish
that shudders like a weak heart.

L M N O

A fine dusting of chalk covered
Mrs. Schneider's hips. My fingers
ached to sketch sheep, rabbits, cottony
fish onto the navy expanse of her backside
whenever I heard her trousers' *whikshuk*
pacing the narrow aisles of desks.
This is where I learned
to conjure opaque ghost-bubbles
out of my milk carton's shredded mouth
with a straw. We sang to the flag
each morning, and the speaker's steel
meshwork would suck up the noise
and funnel our sound back to the government.
We seemed to always be singing:
cows, stars, spiders, and all the boys named Jack.
My name was not in anything.
My favorite moment of our song
of letters was the strange word
that had been dropped in the middle,
a syllabic trill that worked the lips
briskly. O *Ellamennow,* you became
pleasures, dreads, unfurlings:
the collapsed brown divot fouling
the apple, the lingering smell
a penny left in my sweaty fist,
the shimmy of a recoiling pillbug.
Ellamennow, today my father said
that he would never die. *Ellamennow,*
the barber lunged at me with scissors.
Ellamennow, help me learn to tell time
so I can sound important.
Ellamennow, someday when I am old
enough I will jump off of the roof.
Ellamennow, last night I realized
that there are a lot of people
who don't know that I am alive.
Ellamennow, there are too many words.

If no one was watching, *Ellamennow,*
I think I could break from the earth
and rise up into nothing.
Ellamennow, say that I won't.

MY FATHER IS A SMALL SUBMARINE

The hospital room at night
is the bottom of the ocean.
Knotted lengths of clear kelp
tether him to the bed,

and the electric thread of his heart
on the screen becomes a restless eel
questing the coral fan
of the horizontal blinds' shadow.

A half-dozen lionfish,
spines bright with toxins,
have the slow drift of deflating
helium balloons, their sides
inscribed with the rueful maxim
Love Me, Love My Danger.

He clicks the morphine drip,
counting off fathoms.
By dawn, a whale the size
of a housecat will have nestled itself

in the crook of his arm,
conjuring a song
he'll follow into a lightless trench,
a doorstep to the center of the earth.

STILL LIFE WITH HALF-TURNED WOMAN
AND QUESTIONS

after Merwin & Hammershøi

Q. So, what are you working on these days?
    A metaphor machine.

Q. What did you paint first?
    A table that glints with the self-assurance of a rack.

Q. And next?
    A bowl with the pale, rotund mien of a bureaucrat—it's the
        ideal receptacle for a severed head.
    Then bottles, side-by-side, like the hard parallels of a double-
        barreled shotgun.

Q. What's that hanging on the wall, to the left of the table?
    A mirror.
    A window.
    A sliding panel cut in the door of a solitary confinement cell.
    A gray eye gone rectangular with its own blindness.

Q. No really—what's that on the wall?
    Another picture.

Q. Why is she turned away?
    Because she chose to wear the hex on her forehead.
    Because she failed to gleam.
    Because she interrupted.

Q. Why can't you sleep?
    Why can't *you* sleep?

Q. Why can't I sleep?
    Because of all these little unfacings.

VARIATIONS ON THE PHILTRUM

The hollow that divides the upper lip.

i.
Before birth, the angel told a secret
to your mouth, and made the flesh around it blush.
Hushing you up, he pressed a weightless finger
on those naughty lips, denting the flesh above.

ii.
What can separate the odor of instinct
from hot expression but one concave length
of displaced meat more at home in between
fingers or nestled behind distant ears?

iii.
A bare, sensible valley framed by winds
from two northern caverns and a pit yawning
below. No seed stays, no sound hesitates
passing through a place of borrowed shadows.

iv.
In between sense and within sense
there lies a shallow grave dug out for all
the things one hopes you will be wise enough
to lay down, undisturbed, without a word.

MAKO

Motion took on a form
and stayed. No more infatuations
with dried contrails of seagrass
or foam-clotted yards of brine.

I have blundered through liquid
reliquiae in cold niches
of salt and wet. You litter the sea
with unblinking phantoms;

the warmest sea
still cradles these shudders.
Your sleep is little more
than an opiate lingering

in a green-feathered cellar.
The deep lamentations
of coral knuckles and drowned
rosemary remain charmless,

and you have no terror
of the infinite because
you are the infinite.
You were there

at the beginning of water.
Every inch of you is a thresher.
There were nights I dreamed
that you came for me

and blue whispers
drifted out of your breathless mouth.
Once I tied a rock to my ankle
to sing it all back to you.

BLUE THOUGHT/BLUE SHADE

Broad-billed parrot (extinct 17th century)

I flaunt a dense, veinal color, poised
on a bank drained to dull, iron-red dregs.

At my back, a purgatorial mountain
wraps its hips in orange mist.

A shadow cowers underneath my tail.

A mate, I think, would render me less
superb—though solitary, I am, at least,

singular. See how the scrub
nearly faints with admiration.

Every night, the same vision:
overcome by the weight of my head,

I struggle to keep the black barb of this beak
from piercing my own breast.

Every night, I watch
that implacable scythe sink

into a mass of indigo feathers and shear
painlessly through the ribs' curvature
to retrieve my heart,

shrieking back every word I'd taught it.

GENES

Think of them as ornamental, the red beads encircling
the throat of Rembrandt's young woman
at the open half-door, her body monochromed
and shadowed, a single band of light illustrating
a sidelong glance full of distrust. According
to faultless Dutch taste, these are her only ornament
and inheritance, a scattering of blood once idolized
at her mother's breast. Imagine the woman as a girl
on her lap, reaching up to caress the luster
of the cool pellets absently, hardly feeling
each one's little gram of death. And the first time
the daughter saw her laid out while Father
received the neighbors' hard hemispheres
of bread, the only visible thing was a length
of red in the dim room, quietly coiled
in the hollow of one clavicle, modestly satisfied
with the day's work. And although now she hardly
senses their weight at all, she will sometimes feel
at her back, when turning too quickly from the stove,
a distant, heavy tug, as if she were harnessed
to a dark line of those thunderclouds which thickly crowd
the lip of the horizon, but do not shed their rain.

THE DIMINISHING HOUSE

It took us some time to notice. The whole thing could have been going on for weeks beforehand, but this is how it is with neighbors: in exchange for proximity, one maintains a respectful obliviousness. And then one morning we noticed that pieces of gutter edging the house across the street with their bright aluminum buckles were gone, the remaining segments flashing a grin of broken teeth. Next, a window in the upper gable went winking and bare and bashful when its shutter and flowerbox disappeared. *Do-it-yourselfers,* we thought. *Improvements.* The shingles began drifting off in pairs, and eventually the whole roof lay peeled, baring doleful lengths of tarpaper to the sky. We weren't expecting the siding to shrug off all at once the way it did. And then (and this is the part we don't talk about anymore) we started to take little bets about what would be next. *The garage door . . . I've got a feeling. No, you've got it all wrong—the front porch is going to make a break for it.* But then those small, neat breaches in the sheetrock showed up. It wasn't sledgehammer work, we knew—the holes didn't have the irregularity of impact, didn't huff out plaster dust in the sunslants. We finally got the guts to sneak over in the middle of the night and circle the place, stepping carefully around the absent cellar door in the darkness. Every story was riddled with dim perforations, each one letting out its own private sigh when the wind pushed though. When we started to get fuller views of the rooms, we weren't surprised to see the furniture wrapped in bedsheets. But this didn't stay long either, and eventually there was only an easy chair left, holding its two arms out to us from underneath bouquets of laundry-faded flowers.

SEASON OF THE DRUNKEN WASPS

The sun poured its orange jug
into the branches of the distant hill,
a light burying itself in roots,
igniting the trees from within
their grooved xylem-flutes.
All glass is an eye that breaks
itself to blindness, a jagged
swarm of relief . . . even though
the loose panes in the antique hutch
endlessly rattled their warnings,
it took us years to find the sickness
in the house, a stowaway amongst
throw pillows and catchalls.
The night brought haughty ghosts
to our apple trees, disembodied
bodies that plucked the fruit
my mother could not turn into pie
or anything, flung every last one down
to the fermenting earth in disgust—
our acreage turning a surplus
of cider and blank seed
harvested by insects gone
mean and boozy in all six eyes.

LULLABIES

1
I have no keepsake, no charm
against this aphasic moon.
My heart twists backwards to my father;
his shadow cast the first beasts
on the bedroom floor,
and their nightrut still howls up my sleep.
Song and darkness, strung and stored in the same case.
Maker of nightmates and nightmares.
Maker of night. Maker of me.

2
Toad in the yard chokes off a chorus.
Sullen crickets cluster in a shrub,
the sky blank and birddumb.
All I'd needed for stars
was done up in brown constellations
on the spread of his shoulders;
he sang me a fox slaughtering geese,
lovesick murders, a dead man
listening to his lover weep.

3
How his clear tenor and guitar
silvered the mesh on my heart—
from a dozen beds in the years
after his passing, I echoed the chorus
of the saddest summer song:
Let me go home.
I want to go home.
I feel so broke up.
I want to go home.

4
Song from a cut throat:
catgut, sheepgut, woodskin.

Amber body shut up
in a black case that leans hard.
The pick has slipped into the hole
and scratches the balsa like a long-nailed hand.
This tune is what the mind can bear—
a fistful of notes from a mile
of music gone to earth.

5
Child as a junk-daubed thing:
a windfall of shoes and fruitpeel,
a thimble, a matchbox, a wooden spoon
surfacing in the clay.
A bitten ear, a tongue scored with lashes.
O tears for this blood a father
brings his child in a bedtime cup.
O night for a song more lost
than his stilled voice.

6
O you bright nail on which I do my dark unraveling

EROSION

A fossilized car's wreck with a tree spares the beach from total
          anonymity.
How the gastank must have bloomed into the night like a rakish
          handkerchief.
Junk and flotsam and scar tissue bearing witness.
Spare my sight.

Look how the fat droops of woodknots
are like my father's eyes. Look how
they both went to ash in an easy gust.

*

The windchimes in the kitchen were made of stout twigs
and what my father called "mermaids' toenails":
slivers of tumorous glass in white, yellow, peach.

Shells hole-punched and strung, weightless and danglingly sad—
not lost from a neverbody,
but born of beauty and warp,
bastards of moon and rock,
spit up as loose change,
pissed back into the earth like peasant wine,
cursed and questing
for the undanceable feet.

It is the sand and not the sea that takes us.
Why else would it cling so stubbornly to the ravines
and crevices of sun-stripped flesh?
It whispers against the ceramic tiles as we brush our bodies:
let me fill your lungs with my white song.

*

"Let's go feed the duckies."

My head to his hip, skirting the pond,

savoring the reek of free-range gooseshit.
Hand in hand, coaxing indifferent mallards,
dropping pale bread on viscous water.

Kelp clinging to stones.
Myopic carp ovaling
just shy of the meniscus,

heavy and unornamental,
struggling for passage in
a treacherous home.

*There are no legacies but what is looted
from the dead. I crib his throat:
Great Scott, O Excellent, by George—
his timpanic exclamations, my echolalia.*

*

I fed on myths of my father's youth:
he once told me about sitting in the sun,
courting a deep tan for a dance,
and falling asleep, waking swollen,
the lucky grin sapped, the "girlcatcher"
a red and babyfaced Noh mask.
For days, he hid in the dark and burned.

*

A blackened, rippled thumbnail, victim of the rust-headed claw
        hammer:

the blow, the curse,
and his body suddenly fallible.

Workbench under an inch of dust,
and I learned later that dust

was mostly skin—the breakage
of his body was in all its repairs.

Then they carved something out
of his face, leaving a divot of all-new
skin, puckered and rectal pink.
Like he had been touched
by the fingertip of twenty years overnight.
Wounded tissues snowed the trash.
The story of how he was broken.

*

*If the earth learns how
to shine it will flood the frigid
shoreline of the moon with crimson.*

The stars measured him for a box
and they deserve to be ignored.

*

It was the fourth of July and the end of everything.
In the last blue eye of childhood there were unsinging shells and no
    wind.
A searing afternoon and an anonymous seizure on a beachfront road.
And then.

*I revisit the same man's body every day.
No wife or tide is so faithful.*

*

Beachglass has the weary look of a man coming home,

the dusk highlighting the fretwork of his forehead
in a rusted filter, eyes like nickels stacked on half-dollars.

It's the six pm highway,

that leaky seam of light pulling us in marionette chain gangs,
smoothing down our lethal jags,
sapping the green glitter,
whitening first at the jaw,
then the wrist.

Into what did he finally burrow,
what polished his nose away
while sandworms passed him in the grit dark like haunted flatbeds?

CARDINAL VIRTUE

At first, I can't name the bird falling deliberately
from the tree's high crooks: a grey flash, tipped with carmine.
Lit on a fence post, its wings smolder.
It must smell of ginger.
Bird, your life would terrify me.
Bones full of air, belly full of hunger,
the underbrush dense with murders.
Death is a twist, a pinfeather lost,
a stumble over a slowing pebble. This is not a life
of flight, but flight from. Perhaps you don't suppose
that there's any other way, which is itself
a kind of mercy. Perhaps you don't suppose.

Your heart's the size of a small clod and,
so I've heard, egg-shaped. I learned
to measure my own by the scale of my fist,
and my height from the distance
between the forefingers at the ends of my spread arms.
Physical logic is contrast,
ratio, degree. We know desire
by the scarcest shades on our skin:
brief flushes, bitten lips.
How could we sort anything at all
without rarity? There are acres more night
than moon, hours more sleep than dream.

Bird, when you are half-alive
in the jaws of our cats, a yellow ribbon
of innard dragging on the dirt,
remember that we dreamed our radiant dead
would become more like you,
as though the progeny of some impossible
lust between one of ours and one of yours.
Incomprehensible thing, drenched in the color
of something we call joy,
stuffed with something that we call song,
you are always first
inhuman.

OUROBOROS

We are both the snake and the wheel.
—Czeslaw Milosz

Discovered in a New Zealand school's basement:
                                    a colony of garter snakes
twelve inches deep, generations rescrawling
                over themselves within pipe-coiled peripheries,
        the vital graffiti of frigid ardor.

Imagine the plumber's constricted breath,
                                        the dilation of the eye
to accommodate astonishment in the sweating cellar.
                    The snakes' dichromatic diction shifts
        like the changing surface

of beauty's variable dermis. The unquarrelsome bodies yield
        for the chary tread of his gumboots,
                        writhing out a skin-song so elemental
                it renounces all terrestrial sound

to the great flicking tongue of time.
                            Here he came as both the destroyer
        and the distant cousin, his spine thrumming their common
                language
                        of the ancestral notochord: filament of fury
                            and rapture, the enduring, wild
                                thread.

        None truly devours his own tail.   It's always the end
                that endeavors to consume
                                        the beginning—
                    this is the credo of the hole
                            at the end of the world.
        Though he will descend again with other men carrying iron
                shovels,

what will gird the chambers of his sleep
      is the memory of his ankles and wrists
            bound in concentric scaled circles, his flicker
          of life
              within a living hoop of
                eternity,
          the compass of water and air,
          and the earth's innate burning.

HISTORICAL NUDE

Take the head from
the ornament of an Egyptian tomb,
shucked from the unlit millennia,
cordoned-off from the world
beyond the skin
by the most resolute
of charcoal lines—not profile,
but the idea of profile.

The foot will be unsatisfactory
no matter what. Best to dig
one out of the corpse
of the museum, nursery
to a thousand orphaned limbs and end tables.
Since the fire bombing
it has cultivated an entirely new
species of ruin: cloisonné
cigarette holder gripped
in the chilled mineral
of Classical toes.

Let the breasts be rivals:
gather the right from a medieval cornucopia
of nursing virgins, a flat,
red-eyed daisy pressed
into a hymnal. Its Oceanic neighbor's
conical weight will bespeak
a scandalous acquaintance with gravity
and have the florid, weighty polish
of a cocked weapon.

Save the navel for last:
those concave, inscrutable contours
are the first human artifact,
a reliquary of the severed root
leading us out of time.

LOBE OF THE AURICLE

The earlobe.

As it cooled—
that waxy stew He'd mixed with such patience

(and yet how His heart beat still
at the slow thickening of
amber oil, hair, and the seepage of nerve)—

He drifted for a moment, humming,
palate knife and spoon in mid-air,
attendant seraphim in their steely sleeves abiding.

And as whatever lyric nettled that serene brow,
whatever half-done list was fleshed out,
a wayward runnel eked itself
from the labyrinthine conch
and, slipping from that careful bandshell,
pushed out a half-inch
of its own design.

STUMPHUMPER

aka Ichneumonid wasp

An obsidian, Croenenbergian prop,
the horrifying marriage of organic
and engineered, like the hinged, chitinous cunts
of those larval aliens famed for chestbursting.
Landing on the stove, it renders
the rococo contours of the spaghetti spoon
vaguely sinister. Nerve and broom falter:
projecting from its rump are twin stingers,
wickedly black, double the length of its body—
the whole creature nearly half a foot
of vengeance in excess. One cannot
regard it without ruminations of torture—
disembodied hypodermics, bamboo slivers,
fragment of an Iron Maiden's heart—
nor can one ignore the repugnant softnesses
obscured in one's own flesh: small reserves
of future betrayals. But this malevolence of form
is merely that which is female: the doubled barbs
are ovipositors, akin to a snake's split cock—
Nature keen as always to double her productivity—
so that she may seize the pallid, sexless grub, mount
it from behind in the obligatory porno choreography,
and fuck it deeply in the back, filling it
with paradox: an insemination of eggs.
The grub—for whom the open air
is a grave, its life a dim vigil for the incipient,
lacquered salvation of armor and wing
—the grub will take its seclusion in the obliterating
earth, the memory of ravishment dispersing
into bifurcated roots, until all that remains
is a vestigial doubt troubling the placid recesses
of its blind thoughts, easily dismissible, until
the moment when its spine splits and erupts
with life, the young having devoured it
to the immaculate core . . .

In the kitchen, she's buzzing the ceiling fan's
stilled quadrivial. Unimpressed, she jerks
the ink-veined membrane of her wings
in a brief adieu before coasting out the broad,
vertical rent in the window screen,
our femme fatale, an ornate diptych
of double X's against dusk's luminous marquee.

CUBITAL FOSSA

A triangular anatomical region
anterior to the elbow joint.

Pack mule for packages,
cradler of gunbutts,
blackfly cockpit,
cuffcruncher,
nonelbow,
sweat tarn,
gula,
bight.

PROVENANCE

One of the workmen will be pulling down
the old paneling, enjoying how easily
it comes away from the wall, the nails sliding
from their holes with a rusty frisson.
About a yard of plaster will lay bare before
he uncovers what he'll think is wallpaper,
the pattern a faded landscape in miniature,
or the silhouettes of lean clouds over a dune,
or schools of brown eels. But then
he will recognize the word "unyielding," then "thighbone":
your copperplate, some seventy years out of fashion,
slanting across the west and north walls from ceiling
to wainscoting—one hundred poems pasted under the wood,
untitled, separated with microscopic Roman numerals.
It will be a genteel kind of shock, like finding a ghost
who does not know he is a ghost, content to amble
in circles around the same garret, murmuring
mild-mannered exclamations in threadbare shirtsleeves.
You'd done this so that when they came
to take your typewriter, it could go
with them silent and blameless to render
its dutiful cha-cha for a neophyte clerk
with a quiet passion for the stenographer's knees.
It would not be able to say how the city became
a nightmare of starlings, the evening air a plague
of tinny fugues. Or how love was like an orange,
a thing to be stripped with one's fingernails,
split by the seams of its bitter pith and made to weep
a sweetness which burns in the cracked corners
of an open mouth. A ceiling leak had cut a bleeding
trail through your ode to _____, something
all at once *angel and machine, rocking us into dreams*
while the earth splits against history's sullen plow.
You'd named yourself a joiner, a ragpicker,
knitting together a day's scurf into poetry. *One can only be*
sure of the pieces—the whole is the business of God alone.
All our art is dumb luck anyway, a morbid nursery rhyme

of diminishment: for every one of our masterpieces,
there's one rotting to threads behind a screen
in the asylum, one crushed to mortar in the siege,
one blamelessly lost in a street bazaar,
one binding the wound of the heretic,
one in a house burned to its stone roots before the renovations,
consigning us to only the signature of flame.

PATELLAE APOCRYPHA

The kneecaps.

" . . . and so He seeded the earth with stones, and we learned of how we could be torn, crushed, and blocked. And we learned how to despair in this, our life. And in our grief-strewn hours we fell against the hard ground and it did not do us injury. We knelt, and in that kneeling knew of the stone of the body, bone meeting the earthly rock with steadiness. And we first knew of His love . . ."

TO RADIUS AND ULNA

The two bones that form the framework of the forearm.

I sing of arms . . .
From their names alone,
they could have been another pair
of Virgil's jilted:
two slightly horsey,
big-boned sisters
lovesick over the same sailor
who had his hometown
stenciled on one tanned shoulder
in four indigo letters.
Did he take them
separately, hoisting
himself over one white
window sill, then the next,
or did he make it a game,
passing back and forth
between the two of them
at one time in the dark—
restless ship
in a heaving strait—
daring himself to guess
whose leg, whose arm?
What happened next, though,
is certain. The morning
they both found him gone
and the harbor emptied
of burnished masts,
they went down
to the shore.
Ulna, the elder, the homelier,
pulling her shawl over
her head until only the broad,
jutting nose she despised,
that *crow's beak,* was visible.
The younger leaning slightly

on one hip, the tip
of her slipper placed firmly
on the hem
of the other's dress,
as if she were
a plain, slow seabird
caught by the tail . . .
Time and the beach
slowly stuccoed
the pair in a white
mosaic: crabs emptied
and ossified at their feet,
the gulls dropped
guano and feathers,
the sea grass bleached
and wound into their hair.
Each dusk, the sun drowned
a doubled creep of shade
in the tide.

It's nothing
new for anyone to want
this, to be turned
to salt after a night
with someone who seemed
to have it pouring
from his mouth
in marshy lungfuls,
leaching from his fingers
that turned their tongues to paper.
Because we cannot first become
the bull, the swan, the lightning itself
for our loves, we prove
our devotion afterwards
by slowly becoming
unrecognizable.
But these two—they never became

beautiful, no matter what
we may want for them.
Think of how they must have
marveled at their own
stillness,
admired the chaos
that crafts
every quiet thing:
that thin, pale fan
dragged in by the waves
was once the rage of a fish.
This wind-diminished dune
was a mile of sea-roil.
These rocks were fire,
were women
who found,
beneath their tenderness,
an absolute,
an unadorned
yearning for the weight
of a familiar body,
a mute, stolid
lovesong of bones:
to hold.

JUST ABOVE MY CLAVICLES,

I wear a pair of sinkholes   ·
hoisted like a couple on their wedding chairs.

One poet calls them *rainpits*.
In the Song of Songs, they are *the slopes of Gilead*.
And you call them *cisterns of scent*.

There, you hitch your teeth to my shoulder,
warm belly to my cold spine in the nightgrass,
tasting the air in rhythms.

The dark makes you a gap-goer, tether-tongued.
Your fingers crawl me like cavers,
laid flat to the groundskin and inching.

Seek out the folding H's behind my knees,
              the divot at my throat,
              my hair's cool warren for crickets,
              my gullied ribs,
              my buttocks' deft trench.

Notice where I sink into my own flesh,
like a bruise in the nectarine's reddest antipode
where the fruit collapses on its own sweetness.

Love demands a lacuna of the body:
a birdbath for whispers,
some echo-bed for the lover's name.

Love, come kiss me lightly
where I am yoked to a shadow that is not my own.

ODE TO THE PERINEUM

*The area in front of the anus
extending to the genitals.*

O little Purgatory, the necessary expanse
between desire and duty!

THE EXQUISITE FOREPLAY OF THE TORTOISE

Every movement of my body
is a genuflection to stone,
my flesh a chalice for dust,
which is itself the dry ghosts of flesh.

It is true that I have had
my dalliances with the odd
toadstool, the bulbous contours
of their weeping bride-heads,

but oh my love, consider
the rare patience of my desire,
the readiness with which my body
greets you, the anticipation

born in my clay heart
twenty-five years before
I could gaze over the horizon
of your skull, my two legs

trembling on your back
like a ship-born boy's
on his first beach, terrified
he will drown in this strange earth.

for Brian

STILL LIFE, 1656

Runner and bunched white cloth
ruck backwards, revealing
the table's warm length,
the florid shade of a bare,
sun-browned shoulder.

this is how I love you best

A spit-curl
of lemon rind yawns
and droops over the edge.

sun bound in a lean shaft of early window

Amid rude crowds
of oyster shells
a blue-flecked Chinese bowl has forgotten
itself, almost tipping over
in the aftermath of mounting
the broad
serving dish.

bedsheets that imitate your body

Near-drained, the *roemer*
and the trim *façon de Venise* hold
their drams of untasted air,
something silver and not yet breath.

collapsing into their own folds

A bared flank
of cut banquet meat resplendent
in its starched cuff of fat.

this is how adoration moves over flesh

This is how morning touches beloved indolence.

preparing for an annunciation of light

MIDWIFE/MIDSUMMER

Angle the knees apart.

Fat afternoon
for a herd of clouds
pumped with quick lightning.

Make the cut a half-inch wide.

Caterpillar dangles
from honeysuckle tracery
flashing a saffron belly.

Use a new sheet for the blood.

In the ecstasy of air,
a muskrat drags mud-caked
hindquarters against a levee.

Save the membrane for a poultice.

A half-blind woodpecker
batters a sweetgum
while the creek convulses in the downpour.

Slide hands into split flesh and hoist out the cry of all seasons.

SCAPULA

"Shovel." Either of two flat, triangular bones,
each forming the back part of the shoulder in humans;
the shoulder blade.

Cubist in symmetry.
Slice of washed-out meerschaum, part heart-shape,
part crossward-punched fist.
Aerodynamism wasted:
a sail for a small, windless world.

Something I'd made
unknowingly before I had begun
to uncurl into the air.
Who would have thought
I could luminesce?

Some part, residual, which insisted
on imitating angels, or whatever
loose filaments had passed over my eyes—
those vague, skinned-over olives—
in that bag of blood and blackness.

Sometimes I am visited by dreams
of those long months in the womb
when I slowly knitted into stone
ladders and dishes, blindly choosing myself.
Some utterance behind my heart awakens:

Along these inches, the air will move.
This frame will bend around the world,
and the sweetmeats of the eyes and tongue
will build songs around water.
Put your love in your bones,
and shore not your treasures in
the body's walls, for they grow
threadbare, are food for moths.
House love in something that can heal itself,
that will litter the earth

longer than flesh and words,
something the color of faith.

Now you have come to hold me.
If I seem heavy, understand that
I am small and full of old hours.
What epitaph would suffice?
"Here I was touched."

What remains now is a pale, pitted relic
sluicing shadows.

So weigh me gently in one hand, kneel,
and dig a short line into the yielding earth.
Use me to mark a row of new beans.
Let me be a false rock, a cool temple
for anointed earthworms,
an uneven altar for low, quiet prayers.

ANNUAL

I love the inverted interment of summer planting:
burying the to-be-living
while wearing bright yellow gloves
and singing something by Simon and Garfunkel:

I'd rather be the trousers than the belt,
I'd rather be the salsa than the beans,
I'd rather be Manhattan than the Bronx—
that was usually when you'd roll your eyes.

I watched you make deliberate, angled passes
with the mower, a dozen grackles
already at your heels, ravenous
for the churned up nightcrawlers, some in halves.

Cuffs spilling over with cut grass,
you'd scatter throughout the house, and I'd track you
by the loose, drying arrows in the shag.
You've been shearing green sheep again, I'd say.

Two weeks into the spring,
snails and caterpillars turned everything to frail lace.
I became a butcher of small things,
sowing death from a sack of poison pellets.

One night, I turned back
from the garden to the house.
You were silhouetted against the yellow
of the open door,

and I watched you walk the plank
of light along the ground
and step off into the darkness.

This took nearly a year to happen.

A SHORT DOCUMENTARY OF MY FATHER RUNNING BACKWARDS

I want to believe
that during your last
beach road jog,
the seizure
drew you taut;
that you staggered
a few feet in reverse
and threw out
your arms
to the asphalt's firmament
of mica dust and quartz,
the iridescent clouds
of mosquitoes blossoming
from the marshes,
the sunlight's fistful
of broken glass;
that your entire body became
rigid with its own
brightness;
that something quick,
white, and hungry
spied you,
dove,
and fled the earth
with its prize,
so irresistible
was this gleam.

POST-MORTEM

To me, you have bequeathed
a half-dissolved
apple, a spider,
and three crescents
of your fingernails.

A large Y of black stitches
has split your trunk into thirds—
a child's rendition
of a bird migrating
towards your feet.

The arc of the scar
on your right calf
reminds me of a hooked trout
I once saw leaping
from the surge of a stream,

a curve of light shaped
by the moment between life
and the infinite space
just above it.

Smoke-browned fish on a white plate,
dawn-grey body on a silver table—
we do not like to linger
on how the dead may still nourish us.

Later, I will tell your family
what no one ever knew,
but you may have suspected:

you had two exquisite,
plum-colored kidneys,
lustrous and faultless
as the surface of a yolk.

TYPES OF BREATHING

1
There was a time when we wrote
with our own blood. Ground into clay,
the *now* of our flesh mingled
with the *will be* of the earth.

Once we sharpened stones
to bring down quick bodies.
Then we smithed songs to raise them up again:
our enemies rose from our throats
and danced for thousands of years.
In the end, they outlived us.

This language, this sleight-of-hand
juggled up in flimsy alphabets
struggles to name the hardened powder
of our bones, rainbags of soft tissues,
recoiling fields of raw nerve.

Now our imprisoned lungs
grasp at every ingression of air.
*Eupnea, hyperpnea, hyperventilation,
hypoventilation, dyspnea, orthopnea—*
only we could make a pantheon of breathing.

2
Everywhere I can put a word is tinder:
smear of smoke and newsprint.

Every death claims a small dialect.
What I have not told you will go with me.

In our wake, what remains is the body
and the word *body.*

NOTES

"Floating Rib"—The first line is from the poem "War," by Aaron Baker, from his book *Mission Work.*

"Still Life with Half-Turned Woman and Questions"—The poem is based on the works of late 19th-century Danish artist Vilhelm Hammershøi and W. S. Merwin's poem "Some Last Questions."

"Variations on the Philtrum"—The poem's subject is derived, in part, from a scene from the 1995 movie *The Prophecy,* written and directed by Gregory Widen.

"Mako"—The mako is one of the fastest species of all sharks. Reliquae are "remains, as those of fossil organisms" (*Random House Dictionary*).

"Genes"—The poem is based on Rembrandt's *Young Woman at an Open Half-Door,* 1645.

"Lullabies"—The italicized lyrics are from "Sloop John B," traditional, popularized by the Beach Boys.

"Ouroboros"—The ouroboros is the circular symbol of a snake eating its tail. The notochord is a rodlike cord of cells that forms the chief axial supporting structure of the body of lower chordates (such as snakes) and of the embryos of higher vertebrates (such as humans).

"To Radius and Ulna"—Thanks to Maya Gurantz for the gift of an oversized facsimile edition of *Gray's Anatomy* which made the composition of this poem possible.

"Just above my clavicles,"—The poet is Forrest Gander.

"Still Life, 1656"—The poem is based on Willem Claesz Heda's *Banquet Piece with Ham.*

I offer my humble thanks:

To Maya Gurantz and Ben Au, Miles Kahn, Drew Foster, and Beth Nelson for their many, many years of love and support.

To the writers and friends who've influenced so much of the work here: Julie Buchsbaum, Murray Farish, Steve Gehrke and Nadine Meyer, Landon Godfrey and Gary Hawkins, Jennifer Grotz, Sean Hill, Jason Koo, Marc McKee and Camellia Cosgray, Wayne Miller, Pablo Peschiera, Jeff Pethybridge and Carolina Ebeid, Katie Pierce and Mike Kardos, Todd Samuelson, Amy Wilkinson and Nathan Oates, and Alissa Valles.

To my brother, Josh, who makes me proud.

To my wonderful family: the Beers, the Colemans, the Talls, the Salisburys, the Davidsons, the Barkers, and all permutations thereof.

To my generous teachers: Scott Cairns, Mark Doty, Ed Hirsch, Lynne McMahon, J.D. McClatchy, Rod Santos, and Adam Zagajewski.

To Jerry Costanzo, for his faith in my work, and to everyone at Carnegie Mellon University Press for all their work on this book.

To Linda Bierds, for her timely advice.

To the creative writing programs at the University of Houston and the University of Missouri-Columbia. Thanks also to the Unterberg Poetry Center, as well as the Bread Loaf Writers' Conference, and all the friends and mentors met there.

And to Brian Barker, my favorite poet, for giving me my first pair of binoculars and my first animal skull, for his invaluable thoughts on these poems and this book, and for the life we share which makes poetry possible.